COPYRIGHT © MMXXIII ACE KING

D0999187

ACE KING

Notice of Rights:

All rights reserved. No part of this publication may be reproduced, distributed, or transmitted in any form or by any means without the prior written permission of the author. This work is protected under copyright law.

Disclaimer:

This book is intended for entertainment purposes only. The information contained in this book does not constitute legal or financial advice and should never be used without first consulting with a licensed professional. The publisher and the author do not make any guarantee or other promise as to any results that may be obtained from using the contents of this book. You should never make any investment decision without first consulting with your own financial advisor and conducting your own research and due diligence. The author and publisher of this book have used their best efforts in preparing this material. While every attempt has been made to verify information provided in this book, neither the author nor the publisher assumes any responsibility for any errors, omissions, or inaccuracies.

The author and publisher make no representations or warranties of any kind, express or implied, about the completeness, accuracy, reliability, suitability, or availability with respect to this book or the information, products, or services contained within this book. The author and the publisher specifically disclaim any liability that is incurred from the use or application of the contents of this book. The author and publisher shall in no event be held liable for any loss or other damages, including but not limited to any direct, indirect, incidental, consequential, special, or exemplary damage, arising from or in connection with the use of this book or the information contained within this book.

The publisher and the author are providing this book and its contents on an "as is" basis. By reading this book, you agree that the use of the information in this book is at your own risk. If you wish to apply the ideas contained in this book, you take full responsibility for your actions. The author and publisher are not affiliated with OpenAI or ChatGPT.

CHATGPT + AI

FOR ARTISTS

ACE KING

ACE KING

Dedicated, with love, to human brains...

ACE KING

<u>CONTENTS</u>

INTRODUCTION

ACE KING

AI: FRIEND OR FOE?

`"Hello, old friend. . ."`

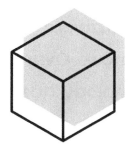

Pick up your smartphone and hold it in your palm. It's not merely a fancy toy made of mirrored glass and metal. It's a window into a world powered by "AI", short for Artificial Intelligence (but I think you knew that by now). Life on Earth has swiftly become a bit like an eerie science fiction film. From the moment we jump out of bed in the morning to check our notifications, to the late night scrolling sessions lit only by a glowing screen, AI algorithms work tirelessly behind the scenes to analyze our preferences, curate personalized content, and make our lives just plain easier. Since the dawn of the smartphone, AI has been right there in our pocket all along, forecasting the weather, setting us up on dates, and sliding hilarious cat videos into our recommendations. "AI" may sound like the buzzword to end all buzzwords, but it's nothing new. Over the course of many years, this technology has steadily become a familiar companion, adapting to our needs, anticipating our desires, and transforming the way we communicate, consume information, and navigate the digital realm.

So why do I keep hearing about ChatGPT?

The introduction of OpenAI's ChatGPT has ignited a profound shift in how mainstream media and everyday individuals perceive and interact with AI due to several huge advancements. More on that later.

Rather than viewing AI as a threat to human creativity, it's better to illuminate its potential to enhance our skills and efficiency. Just like a hammer resting dormant in storage, AI is a tool. A house will _not_ build itself, just like a project will _not_ build itself -- with or without AI's help. The hammer must be put into action, in the correct way, with careful knowledge and understanding. No one in their right mind would go around swinging a hammer in the air and expect a house!

In this book, "ChatGPT + AI for Artists", we'll explore clever ways to utilize Artificial Intelligence with the same approach that countless artists, writers, musicians, and entrepreneurs have used with other groundbreaking inventions throughout history to express themselves and their ideas. Many tools that we now consider to be old fashioned or commonplace were first met with controversy, criticism, and confusion.

Typewriters, analog synthesizers, digital cameras, and the earliest version of the Internet are just a few examples of innovations that transformed the world once the first wave of pioneers embraced and welcomed change.

Contrary to several "doom and gloom" fears about AI replacing imagination while erasing jobs, this book will highlight Artificial Intelligence's potential as a collaborator and muse. AI's capacity to generate novel ideas, assist in business endeavors, automate tasks, and provide fresh perspectives serves as a springboard for inspired action and profitability. With AI's assistance, making a living as an artist and developing a career as a creator has never been easier.

AI can be our friend if we learn how to use it.

ACE KING

CHAPTER ONE

ACE KING

A BRIEF HISTORY

" . . .Chat-what???"

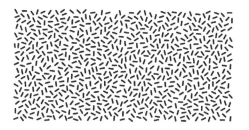

Let's take a moment to learn some specific details that'll get you up to speed.

What exactly *is* ChatGPT?

ChatGPT is a language model developed by OpenAI in San Francisco, California and was first introduced to the public in 2022.

And what is a language model?

Basically, now that there is so much language, text, and information archived on the Internet, a team of specialists were able to figure out how to train software to mimic human speech and to a certain degree, mimic human intelligence.

What does the GPT stand for?

The GPT in ChatGPT stands for "Generative Pre-trained Transformer". Impress your friends!

Isn't ChatGPT the same as other chatbots?

Not even close! What truly sets ChatGPT apart is its generative nature. It goes beyond mere question-answering and pre-written scripts, tapping into its vast knowledge base to generate original and contextually appropriate text. ChatGPT offers users a conversational experience that is rich, expressive, and personalized.

Several key factors contribute to ChatGPT's ability to emulate human-like conversations.

Contextual Understanding:

ChatGPT possesses a deeper understanding of context, allowing it to comprehend and respond to a wider range of inputs. It can maintain context across multiple back-and-forths in a long conversation, resulting in more coherent and relevant responses. ChatGPT is the most naturally conversational chatbot we've seen in history. This contextual awareness enables ChatGPT to engage in more meaningful and natural interactions. It's like talking to an old friend.

Expanded Vocabulary and Knowledge:

ChatGPT has been trained on vast amounts of diverse text data, enabling it to draw from an extensive knowledge base. It can leverage this expansive vocabulary and accumulated knowledge to generate nuanced and informed responses. This breadth of information contributes to its ability to emulate how a person normally speaks, with a diverse range of topics.

Improved Natural Language Generation:

ChatGPT leverages advanced language generation techniques that prioritize fluency and coherence. It employs sophisticated algorithms to produce responses that flow naturally, considering grammar, structure, and semantic coherence. This attention to linguistic quality enhances its conversational capabilities.

Adaptability and Flexibility:

ChatGPT is designed to be adaptable and flexible in its responses. It can handle a wide range of inputs, from casual chit-chat to more complex inquiries. Its ability to adapt to different styles and tones accommodates diverse user preferences and intentions.

Creative Expression and Engagement:

This is a big one. ChatGPT's AI model allows it to generate creative and imaginative responses. It can offer suggestions, insights, and alternative perspectives, fostering an engaging and dynamic conversation. This creativity adds a human-like touch, simulating the diversity of responses one might expect when conversing with another person.

Continuous Learning and Improvement:

ChatGPT benefits from ongoing refinement and updates. It leverages user feedback to enhance its conversational abilities over time. By continuously learning from its interactions, it can improve its responses, becoming more adept at emulating human-like conversation with each iteration.

Future versions and new models are anticipated to push the boundaries of what is possible even further.

What is "The Turing Test" and why is it important?

"The Turing Test" is a concept proposed by mathematician and computer scientist Alan Turing in 1950. The test aims to evaluate a machine's ability to exhibit intelligent behavior that is indistinguishable from that of a human. In the Turing Test, a human judge engages in a natural language conversation with both a machine and another human, without knowing which is which. If the judge cannot consistently determine which is the machine based on their responses, the machine is said to have passed the Turing Test.

While ChatGPT demonstrates impressive language generation capabilities, it's important to recognize that at this time, ChatGPT cannot trick any human into believing it is human. In other words, there is no AI on Earth that is said to have "passed" "The Turing Test". This is an affirmation that AI is a product and service, not a sentient being.

ACE KING

CHAPTER TWO

ACE KING

HOW TO TALK TO AI (PROMPT ENGINEERING 101)

"Nice to E-meet you!"

Before we can dive into specific artistic assignments and activities, we must first become comfortable and familiar with **_how_** to talk to AI in order to get what we want.

Remember the image from earlier of running around while waving a hammer? I'll give you another metaphor. Imagine dumping out a carton of eggs, a jug of milk, and a box of flour onto the kitchen floor. Would you stare longingly at the mess and expect cake? No!

29

What if you found yourself stranded in a foreign country where you didn't speak one word of the language? You'd give anything for a simple translation of basic phrases just so you could find something to eat and a place to sleep!

Similarly, there are special ways we can feed ChatGPT "**prompts**" to grease the wheels of communication and achieve our desired results.

What are "prompts"?

Think of good "**prompts**" like being fluent in AI's language, or having the exact recipe for the perfect cake. Although AI will work with whatever you give it, just like you can throw ingredients on the floor and see what happens, if you give AI thoughtful and well-designed "**prompts**", the results will be much, much better.

People who are very good at coming up with "**prompts**" are called "**prompt engineers**".

This can be you!

Here are some tips to help you craft effective prompts:

Be Clear and Specific:

Clearly state your intention or query in a concise and specific manner. Avoid ambiguity or overly broad statements that might confuse the AI. The more precise your prompt, the more focused and accurate the response is likely to be.

Bad Example Prompt: *"Write a story."*

Good Example Prompt: *"Provide a detailed account from the first person perspective of a travel writer on 10-day adventure in Southeast Asia."*

Provide Context:

Offer relevant context or background information to guide the AI's understanding.

Including key details about the topic, desired outcome, or any constraints can help the AI generate more targeted responses. This contextual information enables the AI model to better comprehend your prompt and generate context-aware replies.

Bad Example Prompt: *"Tell me a book title."*

Good Example Prompt: *"Generate a book title for a detective mystery that would be popular in the 1930's."*

Ask Direct Questions:

Frame your prompts as direct questions whenever appropriate. This guides the AI's response by explicitly requesting the desired information or insights. Clear questions often yield more structured and focused answers, helping you obtain the specific information you seek.

Bad Example Prompt: *"I need a website."*

Good Example Prompt: *"What are the exact steps involved in designing a beautiful website?"*

Set Expectations:

If you have specific requirements or expectations for the response, communicate them clearly in the prompt. For example, if you want a concise summary, ask the AI to provide a summary within a certain word limit. Setting expectations helps the AI understand your desired outcome and tailor the response accordingly.

Bad Example Prompt: *"What is 'Pride and Prejudice' about?"*

Good Example Prompt: *"Write a 500 word scholastic summary of 'Pride and Prejudice.'"*

Experiment and Iterate:

If the initial response doesn't meet your expectations, don't hesitate to iterate and experiment with different phrasings or approaches. Small variations in the prompt can yield different outcomes, so refining and iterating your prompts can lead to more desirable results.

Test Different Strategies:

AI models may respond differently to various prompt strategies. You can try different approaches such as priming the AI with certain information, asking the AI to think step-by-step, or requesting multiple possible solutions. Testing different strategies can help you identify the most effective approach for your specific case.

Good Example Prompt: *"Generate a title for a best-selling novel."*

Alternate Example Prompt: *"Generate a title for an award-winning novel."*

Another Variation: *"Generate a title for a critically-acclaimed novel."*

Get the idea?

As you engage with ChatGPT, learn from its responses, and observe patterns. Refine your prompts based on the AI's strengths and weaknesses, adapting them to optimize the quality of the generated responses over time.

CHAPTER THREE

PROMPTS FOR
SCREENWRITERS + FILMMAKERS

`"Action!"`

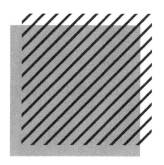

Wouldn't it be great to always have a writing partner with you, at any time of day, to bounce ideas off of? Or what about access to an entire "writer's room" (a team of professional writers all working together to snowball small ideas into big, money-making scripts)? That's how Hollywood operates. How do you think they churn out countless hours of content yearly? Writing alone is like playing tennis alone.

You really need someone on the other side of the net, a tennis partner, to lob the tennis ball back to you. In this same way, writers get the best results when they can "bounce" ideas back-and-forth with one another. This leads to a finished product that is more refined than what one individual could have come up with all by themselves. With each "bounce", the concept changes and evolves. The good news is that AI can act as your writing partner!

AI can help screenwriters and filmmakers brainstorm ideas for plots, characters, and themes. By engaging in a dialogue with the AI, creative suggestions will spark your imagination and lead you down roads you may not have considered had you been writing without any help. Let's explore some examples:

Character Development:

AI chat models can assist in fleshing out characters by providing insights into their backgrounds, personalities, and motivations. Writers can engage in conversations with AI chat models, playing out different scenarios and exploring the depths of their characters' psyche, leading to more nuanced and well-rounded portrayals.

Example Prompt: *"In a thriller film screenplay, what's a one sentence line of action that subtly showcases the villain's motivations are driven by their past?"*

Example Response:

As the villain's eyes fixate on a faded photograph hanging above a locked safe, their trembling hand clenches into a fist, revealing a burning desire for vengeance.

Dialogue Refinement:

AI chat models can be employed to refine and polish dialogue within a screenplay. By interacting with the AI, writers can test the authenticity of their dialogue, receive suggestions for improving the flow or tone, and experiment with different character voices to ensure compelling and engaging conversations.

Example Prompt: *"Respond to this piece of dialog in character as an Edwardian-era chimney sweep: 'Where is the nearest restaurant?'"*

Example Response:

"Ah, well, sir, if ye be seeking a proper establishment to satisfy yer hunger, I reckon by the corner, 'The Crown Pub', might just serve ye well. It's a short stroll down the cobbled streets, with a warm hearth and hearty fare to fill yer belly. Mind ye, sir, mind the soot on me clothes as I guide ye on the way."

Plot Structure and Pacing:

Filmmakers and screenwriters can use AI chat models to analyze and evaluate the structure and pacing of their narratives. By discussing the story arc and plot points with AI, we gain fresh perspectives, identify potential plot holes or inconsistencies, and refine the overall flow of our script.

Example Prompt: *"Provide an easy to understand outline for a movie's three act structure."*

Example Response:

Act 1: Setup

- Introduce the main characters, setting, and establish the story's world.
- Present the protagonist's ordinary life and their desires/goals.
- Introduce the inciting incident that disrupts the protagonist's normalcy.
- The protagonist faces a conflict or

challenge that propels them into
the main story.

Act 2: Confrontation

- The protagonist embarks on a
  journey or faces a series of
  obstacles in pursuit of their goal.
- Rising action builds tension as the
  protagonist encounters conflicts,
  allies, and enemies.
- The midpoint marks a significant
  turning point or revelation that
  changes the protagonist's
  understanding or approach.
- The protagonist faces setbacks,
  confrontations, and personal
  growth.
- The stakes and tension continue to
  escalate.

Act 3: Resolution

- Climax: The protagonist confronts
  the main obstacle or antagonist in
  a decisive, high-stakes encounter.
- The conflict reaches its peak, and
  the protagonist faces a moment of
  truth.
- Falling action: The consequences of

the climax unfold, leading to a resolution.

- The protagonist achieves their goal or undergoes a transformation.
- The story concludes with a sense of closure, tying up loose ends and providing a satisfying resolution.

Worldbuilding and Setting:

AI chat models can help filmmakers and screenwriters in creating vivid and immersive fictional worlds. By engaging in conversations about the environment, culture, and history of their story's setting, they can expand their understanding, gather unique details, and infuse their narratives with depth and authenticity.

Example Prompt: *"On a fictional planet across the universe, which is covered only in oceans, what is the most popular mode of transportation and everyone's favorite food?"*

Example Response:

On the fictional planet of Victory, located on the other side of the universe and covered entirely in vast oceans, the most popular mode of transportation are the sleek and advanced, waterproof hover-ships. These magnificent vessels, equipped with hydrodynamic designs and cutting-edge propulsion systems, navigate the planet's expansive waters with ease, allowing its inhabitants to travel swiftly and smoothly between cities, islands, and underwater realms.

As for everyone's favorite food on Victory, it is the delectable delicacy known as Spicy Ocean Fritters. These scrumptious treats are made from a variety of rare sea vegetables, blended with the finest seasonings from the depths of the ocean. Whether deep-fried or lightly sautéed, Spicy Ocean Fritters offer a delightful burst of flavors.

Wow! Here are some more fun **examples of prompts** you can ask AI when working on a screenplay:

1. *"I require ideas for an engaging opening scene for a thriller set in a small town. What are some intriguing scenarios I could explore?"*

2. *"Can you help me develop a complex and morally ambiguous protagonist for my drama screenplay? What are some personality traits and backstory elements I should consider?"*

3. *"I'm looking to add a plot twist in Act 2 of my mystery script. Can you suggest some unexpected turns or red herrings that could keep the audience guessing?"*

4. *"How can I improve the dialogue between two characters in a romantic comedy? Can you provide some witty banter that captures their chemistry?"*

5. *"I'm struggling with the climax of my action screenplay. Any suggestions for a thrilling set piece that showcases the hero's skills and resolves the main conflict?"*

6. *"What are some unique ways to develop tension and suspense in a horror script? Are there specific techniques or pacing strategies I should consider?"*

7. *"I need help creating an original and visually striking fantasy world for my script. Can you provide some vivid descriptions or cultural elements that could make it come alive on screen?"*

8. *"How can I improve the pacing in Act 1 of my comedy screenplay? Are there any comedic setups or comedic timing suggestions that could enhance the humor?"*

9. *"I'm exploring themes of identity and self-discovery in my coming-of-age script. Can you offer any thought-provoking situations or character dilemmas that could reflect these themes?"*

10. *"What are some effective ways to convey emotions and internal conflicts without relying solely on dialogue in my script? Any visual or symbolic elements I can incorporate?"*

Armed with tons of new and exciting ideas, we may need help formatting the actual script.

Let's see how helpful AI can be with screenplay formatting.

Example Prompt: *"Generate a sample page in the correct format from a comedy sitcom screenplay using two main characters, Mark and Jeff, in a NYC apartment. The scene starts calm and ends in chaos."*

Example Response:

```
FADE IN:


INT.  LIVING ROOM - DAY

Mark sits on the couch, reading a book, while Jeff stands by
the window, sipping a cup of coffee. The room is tidy, and
everything appears calm.

                    MARK
          You know, Jeff, sometimes I feel like
          life couldn't get any more
          predictable.


                    JEFF
               (smiling)
          I know what you mean, Mark. It's like
          we've finally found some peace in
          this crazy city.

Suddenly, a loud crash is heard from the kitchen, followed
by a series of clattering sounds. Mark and Jeff exchange
worried glances.

                    MARK
          What was that?

                    JEFF
          I have no idea, but it doesn't sound
          good.

They rush into the kitchen, finding Peter frantically trying
to control a small fire on the stove. Smoke fills the room,
and chaos ensues.

                    MARK
               (panicked)
          Peter, what did you do?

                    PETER
               (frantically waving a
                towel)
          I was just trying to make toast, and
          things got out of hand!

Mark and Jeff spring into action, spraying a fire
extinguisher and managing to extinguish the flames. The room
is now covered in a layer of white foam.

                    MARK
          Well, that escalated quickly.
```

As you can see, AI did a great job getting us started! The AI even introduced a new third character, Peter, into the equation, which we may not have thought of ourselves. Where did Peter come from and why was he making toast? How will these three explain this to the landlord? From here, we can continue to feed ChatGPT prompts, or continue the script manually. In just a few seconds, we were able to examine what a simple idea looks like in the official screenplay format, since AI is an expert at formatting.

Example Prompt:

"Generate 25 potential locations for two characters to meet and fall in love."

Example Response:

1. A bustling coffee shop in a vibrant city

2. A picturesque park with blooming cherry blossoms

3. A charming bookstore with cozy reading nooks

4. An art gallery showcasing an experimental exhibition

5. A serene beach at sunset

6. A lively music festival in a huge park

7. A charming small-town bakery with irresistible treats

8. A hiking trail with breathtaking mountain views

9. A friend's birthday party at a local restaurant

10. A dance studio overlooking midtown Manhattan

11. An exotic garden with blooming flowers and enchanting pathways

12. A vintage record store with a hidden treasure of vinyl records

13. A food festival with cuisines from around the world

14. A cozy cabin in the woods, surrounded by nature's beauty

15. A rooftop bar during a display of fireworks

16. A historic museum where their shared interests align

17. A shopping mall filled with tourists

18. A romantic garden with cascading flowers and twinkling lights

19. A charming lakeside pier where they bond over their love of sailing

20. A scenic vineyard with rolling hills as far as the eye can see

21. A whimsical carnival with thrilling rides and nostalgic fun

22. A hidden waterfall in a secluded forest, offering a peaceful retreat

23. An outdoor theatrical performance, under a blanket of stars

24. A haunted hotel on a stormy night

25. A botanical garden with colorful flowers and tranquil ponds

These locations provide a backdrop for romance to bloom, capturing the essence of different settings that can ignite a deep connection and spark love between two characters.

CHAPTER FOUR

PROMPTS FOR VISUAL ARTISTS, PAINTERS, + DESIGNERS

"A picture is worth a thousand words"

AI can serve as a powerful catalyst for visual artists, painters, and designers. I'll let you in on a little secret. We can ask ChatGPT to give _us_ prompts! That's right! ChatGPT can act as an art teacher handing out homework assignments and _we_ are the students! Don't worry! I'm not talking about math homework. Art homework is sometimes what us artists

59

need in order to spark our genius. Specific challenges force us to put on our thinking hats and become creative problem solvers. Ever notice how you might be staring at a blank page without a clue as to what to draw or where to begin? Yet, if someone was standing beside you and said, "Draw a clown cat on stilts!", a million random ideas would come out of nowhere! It's funny how that works. Assignments motivate us by giving us concrete directions within a framework. Think of art homework from your new art teacher, professor ChatGPT, like a game or puzzle where you can exercise your mind and have fun, while also honing your craft.

Example Prompt: *"List 50 prompts for visual artists, painters, and designers that inspire action and get the creative juices flowing!"*

Example Response:

1. Generate a surreal landscape merging elements of the ocean and the cosmos.

2. Create an abstract composition inspired by the concept of harmony.

3. Design a logo for a fictional tech company that represents innovation and connectivity.

4. Combine vibrant colors and geometric shapes to create a visually striking pattern.

5. Illustrate a scene from a classic novel with a modern and imaginative twist.

6. Generate a portrait that captures the essence of someone's personality without showing their face.

7. Design a book cover for a fantasy novel set in a mythical forest.

8. Create a series of minimalist illustrations depicting the four seasons.

9. Generate a futuristic cityscape that showcases eco-friendly technologies.

10. Design a tattoo incorporating elements of nature and spirituality.

11. Create an illustration inspired by your favorite song, evoking its mood and lyrics.

12. Generate a still life composition featuring a unique arrangement of everyday objects.

13. Design a poster for a music festival, incorporating elements from various music genres.

14. Create a digital painting inspired by a childhood memory that holds emotional significance.

15. Generate a whimsical illustration of anthropomorphic animals engaged in a lively tea party.

16. Design a pattern inspired by the intricate details of a specific cultural tradition.

17. Create a digital collage that blends vintage photographs with modern elements.

18. Generate a series of illustrations exploring the theme of identity and self-expression.

19. Design a cover for a fashion magazine featuring bold typography and striking imagery.

20. Create abstract artwork inspired by the movement of water.

21. Generate a psychedelic poster for a music concert, inspired by 1960's counterculture.

22. Design a logo for an organic skincare brand, emphasizing natural ingredients and sustainability.

23. Create an illustration inspired by a famous myth or legend from a different culture.

24. Generate a digital painting depicting the beauty and diversity of marine life.

25. Design a mural for a community space that celebrates unity and cultural diversity.

26. Create a series of character illustrations inspired by different art movements throughout history.

27. Generate an album cover for a jazz record, capturing the improvisational and soulful nature of the music.

28. Design a poster promoting environmental awareness and the importance of conservation.

29. Create a portrait using only geometric shapes and patterns.

30. Generate an illustration depicting a futuristic city where nature and technology coexist harmoniously.

31. Design a label for a healthy snack company that reflects its unique flavor.

32. Create a digital painting capturing the energy and excitement of a bustling city at night.

33. Paint a portrait inspired by the concept of dreams and the subconscious mind.

34. Design a logo for a charity organization dedicated to helping families in need.

35. Create an illustration depicting a whimsical underwater world filled with mythical creatures.

36. Generate a poster for a film festival, incorporating iconic imagery from classic movies.

37. Design a pattern inspired by the intricate architecture of a historical landmark.

38. Create a series of illustrations capturing the essence of different music genres.

39. Draw a scene inspired by a famous quote, representing its meaning visually.

40. Design a magazine spread exploring the theme of body positivity and self-acceptance.

41. Create a digital painting depicting the vastness and beauty of outer space.

42. Generate an illustration depicting a futuristic transportation system inspired by nature.

43. Design a logo for an artisanal coffee shop that emphasizes craftsmanship and quality.

44. Create a series of illustrations inspired by different cultural celebrations and festivals.

45. Generate a surreal artwork blending elements of nature and technology in unexpected ways.

46. Design a poster for a theater production, capturing the essence of the play's themes and mood.

47. Create an illustration inspired by a specific art movement, reimagining it with a modern twist.

48. Generate an abstract composition using unconventional materials and textures.

49. Design a packaging concept for a luxury chocolate brand, combining elegance and indulgence.

50. Create a collage merging photographs from around the world, representing global diversity.

Try it yourself!

Ask ChatGPT to give _you_ a list of prompts and start creating!

ACE KING

CHAPTER FIVE

CAN MUSICIANS USE CHATGPT? (HINT: YES!)

`"If music be the food of love, play on"`

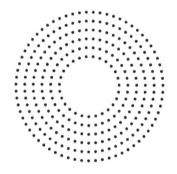

Making music might seem like a strange thing to ask AI to help you with, but it's not! Let's look at some ways musicians can benefit from ChatGPT.

Example Prompt: *"Explain the structure of an award-winning #1 hit pop song."*

Example Response:

1. <u>Introduction (Verse 1)</u>: The song typically starts with an introduction that sets the tone and captures the listener's attention. It often includes instrumental elements or a short vocal phrase to establish the musical backdrop.

2. <u>Verse 1</u>: The first verse introduces the story or theme of the song. It lays the foundation for the lyrics and provides context for the chorus.

3. <u>Pre-Chorus</u>: The pre-chorus, also known as the build-up or lift, usually comes after the first verse. It serves as a transition from the verse to the chorus, often increasing in intensity and building anticipation.

4. <u>Chorus</u>: The chorus is the most memorable and catchy part of the song. It typically features a strong, melodic hook that is repeated multiple times throughout the song. The chorus often delivers the main message or emotional core of the song and is designed to be easily singable and memorable.

5. <u>Verse 2:</u> Following the first chorus, the second verse continues to develop the story or theme, adding new lyrics or building upon the initial ideas. It may have similar or slightly different musical arrangements compared to the first verse.

6. <u>Pre-Chorus:</u> Similar to the first pre-chorus, this section serves as a build-up leading into the second chorus.

7. <u>Chorus:</u> The second chorus is usually a repeat of the first chorus, reinforcing the main hook and message of the song.

8. <u>Bridge:</u> The bridge provides a contrast to the rest of the song. It often introduces new melodies, chord progressions, or lyrical content. The bridge can add emotional depth, create a sense of tension or release, or provide a new perspective on the song's theme.

9. <u>Final Chorus:</u> After the bridge, the final chorus is often more impactful, incorporating elements from previous sections or adding new musical elements to create a sense of climax and resolution.

10. <u>Outro:</u> The outro serves as the conclusion of the song, gradually fading out or providing a definitive ending. It may feature instrumental sections, vocal ad-libs, or a repeat of the chorus, depending on the song's style.

Nice! It's worth noting that this structure can be flexible, and different songs may deviate from this format or incorporate additional sections like pre-verse, post-chorus, or instrumental breaks. Successful pop songs often balance familiarity and catchy hooks with unique elements and creative twists to captivate listeners and stand out in a competitive industry.

Now that we understand structure, let's ask AI for an even clearer example using lyrics.

Example Prompt: *"Generate lyrics for a powerful song about falling in love in the previously explained structure."*

Example Response:

Verse 1:

In a crowded room, our eyes first met, a spark ignited, a love I won't forget.

Your smile, like sunshine, brightened up my day, I couldn't help but feel your love coming my way.

Pre-Chorus:

Every heartbeat, it's getting louder. This connection, it's getting stronger.

Chorus:

I'm falling, falling into your embrace, lost in love, in this enchanting space.

You're the fire that sets my soul ablaze, with every touch, I'm lost, with every touch, I'm lost.

Verse 2:

With every word you speak, I'm captivated, the way you understand me, it's like we're fated. In your arms, I find solace and peace, this love we share, it feels so sweet.

Pre-Chorus:

Every moment, it's a thrill, our love's a symphony, soaring to new heights.

Chorus:

I'm falling, falling into your embrace, lost in love, in this enchanting space.

You're the fire that sets my soul ablaze, with every touch, I'm lost, with every touch, I'm lost.

Bridge:

In this love story, we'll dance through the night, together we'll conquer any darkness or fight. Our love's a wildfire, burning bright and strong, with you by my side, I know where I belong.

Chorus:

I'm falling, falling into your embrace, lost in love, in this enchanting space.

You're the fire that sets my soul ablaze, with every touch, I'm lost, with every touch, I'm lost.

Outro:

We'll chase dreams together, hand in hand, forever.

We'll face the highs and lows, our story truly glows.

You can now edit and modify these lyrics as you see fit.

Did you ever wish you could have a talent agent and music manager at your fingertips?

Unlike certain websites which present information in an encyclopedic format, or a search engine, which provides a vast sea of cluttered results, ChatGPT distills complex information into concise, actionable tips. It goes beyond surface-level details and comprehends the heart of the matter, presenting you with practical insights that resemble a nuanced correspondence.

Musicians can seek guidance on various aspects of their music career, including marketing and promotion, branding, tour planning, and industry trends. By asking specific questions and providing context, musicians can receive tailored advice. ChatGPT can offer recommendations on effective social media strategies, identify potential collaborations, and provide tips for building a loyal fanbase.

Example Prompt: *"What are exact steps an independent singer/songwriter can take to promote their music and get signed by a major label?"*

Example Response:

1. Create High-Quality Recordings:

Invest in professional-quality recordings of your songs. A well-produced and polished sound can make a significant impact on listeners.

2. Build an Online Presence:

Establish a strong online presence through social media platforms, a website, and music streaming platforms. Share your music, engage with fans, and showcase your unique brand and personality.

3. Grow Your Fanbase:

Focus on building a dedicated fanbase by performing live shows, connecting with your audience, and leveraging social media to engage with fans. Regularly release new music to keep your fans engaged and attract new listeners.

4. Collaborate and Network:

Collaborate with other musicians, producers, and songwriters to expand your network and gain exposure to new audiences. Attend industry events, workshops, and conferences to connect with professionals and fellow artists.

5. Seek Media Coverage:

Approach music blogs, local newspapers, magazines, and online publications to secure coverage and reviews. Submit your music to relevant playlists and radio stations to broaden your reach.

6. Utilize Music Licensing and Sync Opportunities:

Explore opportunities to license your music for film, TV, commercials, and video games. Licensing can provide valuable exposure and generate income.

7. Seek Professional Representation:

Consider partnering with a music manager or booking agent who can help navigate the industry, secure gigs, and create strategic partnerships.

8. Submit to Major Labels:

Research major labels that align with your musical style and audience. Study their submission guidelines and follow the proper channels to submit your music. Personalize your approach and highlight your unique selling points.

9. Leverage Industry Showcases and Competitions:

Participate in industry showcases, talent competitions, and music festivals to gain exposure and catch the attention of industry professionals, scouts, and label representatives.

Great! Now it's time to rock!

CHAPTER SIX

THE POWER OF POETRY WITH AI

`"What immortal hand or eye. . ."`

ChatGPT can educate us in a way that is similar to working with a private tutor. Almost unbelievably, AI can guide us towards workshopping poems.

Example Prompt:

"What is an example of a complex rhyme scheme?"

Example Response:

An example of a complex rhyme scheme is the Shakespearean Sonnet, also known as the English Sonnet. It follows a specific pattern of rhymes throughout its 14 lines. The rhyme scheme of a Shakespearean Sonnet is typically represented as ABAB CDCD EFEF GG.

Shall I compare thee to a summer's day? (A)

Thou art more lovely and more temperate: (B)

Rough winds do shake the darling buds of May, (A)

And summer's lease hath all too short a date: (B)

Sometime too hot the eye of heaven shines, (C)

And often is his gold complexion dimmed; (D)

And every fair from fair sometime declines, (C)

By chance or nature's changing course untrimmed: (D)

But thy eternal summer shall not fade (E)

Nor lose possession of that fair thou owest; (F)

Nor shall Death brag thou wander'st in his shade, (E)

When in eternal lines to time thou growest: (F)

So long as men can breathe or eyes can see, (G)

So long lives this, and this gives life to thee. (G)

Each letter represents a different end rhyme sound. The pattern remains consistent throughout the sonnet, alternating between different rhyme sounds, until the final couplet, where both lines end with the same sound (GG).

Wow! What a great, concise lesson from ChatGPT!

Now, let's really use the power of AI and take it one step further. Time to get creative!

Example Prompt: *"Generate a Shakspearean sonnet about a fox, an electric guitar, and a snowman."*

Example Response:

In winter's grasp, where snowflakes softly fall, (A)

A cunning fox emerges from the trees, (B)

With nimble steps, it heeds the frosty call, (A)

While moonlight dances on the snowy lees. (B)

Its fiery eyes, a spark of mischief gleam, (C)

As it approaches a forgotten scene, (D)

An electric guitar, a forgotten dream, (C)

```
Now buried 'neath the snow's crystalline sheen. (D)

 But hark! The fox, with playful curiosity, (E)

 Unearths the instrument with gentle paws, (F)

   And in the moonlit night, a melody (E)

  Resounds, defying winter's icy laws. (F)

A snowman bears witness to the fox's serenade, (G)

  And the fox and snowman dance unafraid. (G)
```

Amazing! We can continue to input new topics for new poems. Have fun coming up with unusual combinations.

With an increased understanding of how to structure this style, we can now more easily work on poems in this rhyme scheme from scratch.

Let's try working as a team with ChatGPT. In this next prompt, we'll let ChatGPT get us started, but it will be our own personal goal to finish the piece.

Example Prompt: *"Generate an ABAB rhyme scheme poem, but leave some words blank."*

Example Response:

```
In the _____ of twilight, where shadows dance,(A)

   A _____ of hope paints the evening sky, (B)

   Whispering winds, a playful, mystic trance, (A)

        As nature's voice sings a lullaby. (B)

Beneath a _____ of stars, shimmering bright, (A)

           A _____ of dreams, (B)

   Silent wishes, like fireflies in flight, (A)

     Illuminate _____, reflective beams. (B)

With each _____ we take, we find our way, (A)

In this _____ of life, a bittersweet song, (B)

     Embracing the unknown, come what may, (A)

With courage and _____, we journey along. (B)
```

These sorts of exercises can really get the wheels in our brain turning!

ChatGPT is useful for seasoned poets as well as beginners.

Example Prompt: *"What are 8 ways poets can earn an income and make a living with their craft?"*

Example Response:

1. Publishing:

Traditional publishing or self-publishing poetry collections can generate revenue through book sales. Explore publishing options and consider submitting your work to literary magazines, anthologies, or online platforms that offer compensation for accepted poems.

2. Poetry Contests:

Participating in poetry contests can provide opportunities to win cash prizes, publication, or other forms of recognition. Keep an eye out for reputable poetry competitions and submit your best work.

3. Performance and Readings:

Poets can earn income by performing their poetry at public events, open mic nights, or poetry slams. You might charge an entrance fee, sell merchandise (such as books or shirts), or receive payment for your performance.

4. Workshops and Teaching:

Share your expertise by conducting poetry workshops or teaching poetry classes. This can be done online or in-person, and you can charge a fee for participants to attend. You may also consider working as writer-in-residence at schools or universities.

5. Writing Grants and Fellowships:

Research and apply for grants and fellowships specifically tailored for poets. These programs provide financial support and often come with opportunities for public readings, collaborations, or artistic development.

6. Literary Magazines and Online Platforms:

Submit your poems to literary magazines or online platforms that offer payment for published work. Some publications pay contributors for their poetry, providing both exposure and compensation.

7. Collaborations and Commissions:

Collaborate with artists, musicians, or other creatives to create interdisciplinary projects that combine poetry with other art forms. Additionally, you can offer commissioned poems for special occasions like weddings, anniversaries, or other personalized requests.

CHATGPT + AI FOR ARTISTS

8. Crowdfunding:

Allows supporters to contribute financially in exchange for exclusive content, behind-the-scenes access, or personalized poems. Crowdfunding platforms can also help fund specific poetry projects.

Well done, ChatGPT! Are there other ways we can profit as artists? Turn to the next chapter to learn more!

CHAPTER SEVEN

MONETIZING CREATIVITY
(ART AS A BUSINESS)

"Inside an acorn hides a forest"

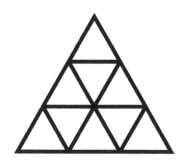

You have the power to use your natural talents to make a living! Forget the phrase "starving artist" immediately! Banish it from your vocabulary. Being an artist can be as profitable as any other profession. It is a worthwhile and noble pursuit. Focus on viewing your surroundings with a career-oriented mindset.

Be open to new ways you can provide value to your community, other businesses, and the world.

Engage in conversations with ChatGPT to brainstorm ideas for new products and services. Ask open-ended questions and explore different perspectives to spark innovative thinking.

Concept Development:

Collaborate with ChatGPT to develop and refine concepts for your business. Describe your vision, target audience, and desired outcomes, and let ChatGPT provide insights, suggestions, and alternative angles to help you shape your ideas.

Branding and Marketing:

Use ChatGPT to explore creative branding strategies, taglines, and marketing campaigns. Seek input on how to convey your business's values, story, and unique selling points in a compelling and artistic manner.

Let ChatGPT provide suggestions and inspiration for logos, websites, packaging, color schemes, aesthetics, or any other aspects of your business.

Storytelling:

Harness ChatGPT's storytelling abilities to craft engaging narratives around your products or services. Create a captivating and memorable brand identity.

Problem Solving:

Describe the challenges or obstacles you face in your business, and seek alternative perspectives or out-of-the-box solutions from ChatGPT. ChatGPT can offer fresh insights and unconventional approaches.

Critically evaluate and adapt the generated ideas to align with your goals and objectives.

Think like an artist while maintaining a pragmatic entrepreneurial spirit.

While traditional methods of selling artwork, such as galleries and art fairs, are well-known, there are alternative avenues that artists can explore to sell their work.

Example Prompt: *"What are ways artists can sell their work that the average artist might not know about?"*

Example Response:

1. Online Art Platforms:

Utilize online art marketplaces and platforms specifically designed for artists to sell their work. These platforms provide a global reach, allowing artists to showcase and sell their pieces to a wide audience.

2. Social Media Presence:

Build a strong presence on social media platforms. Share high-quality images of your artwork, engage with followers, and use relevant hashtags to reach potential buyers. Consider partnering with influencers or collaborating with other artists to expand your visibility.

3. Art Licensing:

Explore the world of art licensing, where your artwork can be used on various products, such as home decor, stationery, or apparel. Licensing agreements can provide ongoing revenue streams and exposure to new audiences. Research art licensing agencies or connect directly with manufacturers interested in licensing unique designs.

4. Art Rental Services:

Offer your artwork for rent through art rental services or agencies. These platforms connect artists with individuals or businesses looking to display art on a temporary basis. Art rentals provide exposure, potential sales opportunities, and recurring income.

5. Corporate and Hospitality Commissions:

Research corporate clients and hospitality establishments, such as hotels, restaurants, and offices, for commissioned artwork. Develop a portfolio showcasing your ability to create custom pieces that suit their aesthetic and branding requirements. Network with interior designers, architects, or art consultants who specialize in such projects.

6. Pop-up Exhibitions and Collaborations:

Organize or participate in pop-up exhibitions or collaborative events with other artists, local businesses, or community organizations. These events provide exposure to new audiences and create a unique atmosphere for showcasing and selling artwork.

7. Art Auctions and Fundraisers:

Contribute artwork to charity auctions or fundraisers. Not only does this support a good cause, but it also exposes your work to potential collectors and art enthusiasts attending the event.

8. Online Courses and Workshops:

Share your artistic expertise and knowledge by offering online courses, workshops, or tutorials. This allows you to generate income while establishing yourself as an authority in your field, potentially leading to sales of your artwork or commissions.

By exploring these alternative avenues, artists can tap into new opportunities, reach a broader audience, and enhance their sales potential. It's essential to research and experiment with various methods to find the ones that align with your artistic style, target market, and long-term objectives.

Example Prompt:

"Generate 40 business tips for artists who want to be profitable doing what they love."

Example Response:

1. Define your target market and tailor your artwork to their preferences.

2. Develop a strong and cohesive brand identity.

3. Create a professional portfolio showcasing your best work.

4. Invest in high-quality promotional materials, such as business cards and brochures.

5. Build a professional website to showcase and sell your artwork.

6. Constantly experiment with new techniques and mediums to expand your artistic range.

7. Collaborate with other artists or businesses for mutual promotion.

8. Attend art fairs, exhibitions, and networking events to connect with potential buyers.

9. Offer limited edition prints or reproductions of your artwork.

10. Develop a pricing strategy that reflects the value of your artwork.

11. Research and apply for art grants and funding opportunities.

12. Create a mailing list and send regular newsletters to your subscribers.

13. Stay up to date with industry trends and incorporate them into your work.

14. Participate in juried exhibitions to gain exposure and recognition.

15. Leverage online marketplaces and platforms for wider reach.

16. Implement effective SEO strategies to increase visibility online.

17. Seek opportunities for public art installations or collaborations.

18. Develop partnerships with local businesses for showcasing and selling your artwork.

19. Offer customization options to appeal to individual preferences.

20. Develop relationships with art galleries for potential representation.

21. Provide exceptional customer service to build loyalty and word-of-mouth referrals.

22. Consider offering a range of price points to cater to different budgets.

23. Use professional product photography to showcase your artwork accurately.

24. Offer flexible payment options, including installment plans or layaway.

25. Regularly update and diversify your portfolio to attract repeat buyers.

26. Seek press coverage and media features to increase exposure.

27. Stay organized with your finances, including tracking expenses and sales.

28. Collaborate with local charities or nonprofits for fundraising events.

29. Offer limited-time promotions or discounts.

30. Participate in online art auctions or sales events.

31. Create engaging video content showcasing your artistic process.

32. Network with industry professionals, art critics, and influencers.

33. Stay true to your artistic vision and maintain consistency in your style.

34. Continuously improve your skills through workshops, courses, or self-study.

35. Seek out feedback and constructive criticism to grow as an artist.

36. Explore alternative revenue streams, such as promotional merchandise.

37. Monitor and analyze your sales data to identify patterns and trends.

38. Stay connected with your audience through regular updates.

39. Develop a strong online presence beyond social media, such as a blog or podcast.

40. Stay motivated, persistent, and passionate about your art, even during challenging times.

Nice! Thank you, AI!

Remember, every artist's journey is unique, so adapt these tips to fit your specific goals and circumstances.

CHAPTER EIGHT

CONQUERING "WRITER'S BLOCK" WITH CHATGPT

"Open the flood gates. . ."

We have now learned many powerful ways to use AI as a writing partner, coach, and launchpad for brainstorming.

"Writer's block" can be a pesky challenge that just won't quit. If at any point you still feel creatively stuck, try asking AI bluntly about ways to defeat this.

Example Prompt:

"Create an action plan for an artist who has writer's block."

Example Response:

1. Acknowledge and Accept the Block:

Understand that experiencing writer's block is a normal part of the creative process. Avoid getting frustrated or overly critical of yourself. Acceptance will help you approach the situation with a more positive mindset.

2. Freewriting:

Set aside dedicated time to write without worrying about grammar, structure, or coherence. Let your thoughts flow freely, allowing your creativity to take over. This can help break through mental barriers and spark new ideas.

3. Change of Environment:

If you usually write in the same place, try moving to a different environment. A change of scenery can provide a fresh perspective and stimulate your creativity.

4. Take Breaks and Relax:

Sometimes, stepping away from your writing for a while can help clear your mind. Engage in activities that relax and recharge you, such as going for a walk, practicing mindfulness, or pursuing a hobby. This can rejuvenate your creative energy.

5. Set Realistic Goals:

Break down your writing tasks into smaller, manageable goals. Setting achievable targets can help alleviate the pressure and make the writing process less overwhelming.

6. Seek Inspiration from Others:

Surround yourself with sources of inspiration. Read books, articles, or poetry in your genre or explore different art forms. Engaging with other creative works can trigger new ideas and perspectives.

7. Eliminate Distractions:

Create a conducive writing environment by minimizing distractions. Turn off notifications on your devices and find a quiet space.

8. Establish a Routine:

Set a regular schedule for your creative practice. Create a designated workspace.

9. Embrace Imperfection:

Remember that first drafts don't have to be perfect. Give yourself permission to write without judgment or self-criticism. Editing and refining can come later.

Remember, writer's block is a common hurdle that many writers face. Every artist experiences periods of creative stagnation. Be patient with yourself, try different strategies, and find what works best for you.

Example Prompt:

"List 50 things artists can do to gather new ideas without the use of a computer or phone."

Example Response:

1. Take a walk in nature.

2. Visit an art museum or gallery.

3. Read books from different genres.

4. Write in a journal.

5. Practice meditation or mindfulness.

6. Attend local art exhibitions or events.

7. Engage in physical exercise.

8. Experiment with different art mediums like paint, clay, or collage.

9. Try a new recipe and cook a meal from scratch.

10. Visit a local library and browse through different books.

11. Take a day trip to a nearby city.

12. Practice yoga or stretching.

13. Spend time observing people in a public space.

14. Take a photography walk and capture interesting scenes.

15. Listen to music from different genres or cultures.

16. Engage in DIY crafts or upcycling projects.

17. Visit a botanical garden.

18. Explore a nearby park or hiking trail.

19. Attend a live theater performance or concert.

20. Rearrange your room.

21. Explore a local flea market or antique store.

22. Practice sketching or doodling.

23. Volunteer for a cause you care about.

24. Learn to play a musical instrument.

25. Take a dance class.

26. Visit a historical site.

27. Attend a workshop or seminar on a topic of interest.

28. Try your hand at calligraphy.

29. Explore different historical landmarks in your town.

30. Start a small garden or tend to houseplants.

31. Practice deep breathing exercises.

32. Visit a coffee shop and people-watch.

33. Engage in a puzzle or brain-teaser activity.

34. Start a collection of interesting objects or artifacts.

35. Learn about art and traditions from different cultures.

36. Experiment with different forms of poetry, like haiku or sonnets.

37. Attend a local community event or festival.

38. Visit a local farmers market.

39. Take a scenic drive to a nearby countryside.

40. Color in a coloring book.

41. Engage in a sensory experience like tasting different teas or chocolates.

42. Try pottery or ceramics.

43. Take up knitting, crocheting, or embroidery.

44. Write letters or cards to friends or family.

45. Sing.

46. Visit a local zoo or aquarium.

47. Watch a sunrise or sunset.

48. Explore different genres of films or documentaries.

49. Visit a local library.

50. Engage in reflective or philosophical thinking.

Remember, these activities are not only great for gathering new ideas but also for personal growth, relaxation, and expanding your horizons. Enjoy the process!

CLOSING THOUGHTS

IS HUMAN-MADE ART
IN DANGER?

`"I'm sorry, Dave. . ."`

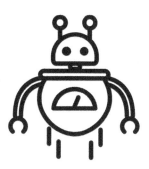

Could we one day wake up in a world where AI produces _all_ of our movies, TV, books, magazines, music, games, and everything else?

What if, for example, instead of searching for a pre-made TV series on a popular streaming platform, you simply type in the story you wish to see and press play?

Will human-made art created exclusively by human artists (without any help from AI) still exist in the future? It's a weird question, but one we must ponder.

As you've now seen, Artificial Intelligence holds immense promise, offering remarkable potential for advancements in various fields and the betterment of human life. While concerns and fears surrounding AI's rapid progress and its implications are understandable, it is crucial to approach the subject with a balanced perspective. Rather than succumbing to undue panic, it is more productive to embrace the possibilities AI presents and work towards responsible development.

AI-driven automation has the potential to alleviate humans from mundane, repetitive tasks, allowing us to focus on higher-level decision-making. This shift will redefine "work" as we know it, and free up time for pursuing meaningful thinking that only humans can do.

Issues such as job displacement necessitate careful consideration and proactive measures. Safeguards, regulations, and transparency must be established to ensure AI is deployed responsibly. The collaborative efforts of policymakers, researchers, industry experts, and society as a whole are instrumental in shaping the trajectory of AI. And this includes you!

Discussions about AI's ethical frameworks, legal frameworks, and guidelines are imperative. We can leverage the collective wisdom to shape a future where AI is a force for good.

It's important to remember that AI is a tool created by humans and remains under human control. As we continue to advance AI technologies, it is our responsibility to imbue them with our values and a shared vision of a better future.

Artistic expression involves (sometimes painful) emotions, memories, loss, love, desire, and a vast spectrum of individual experiences which are intrinsically human. Artists use their work to communicate feelings, raise awareness, surprise one another, entertain friends, engage in social commentary, promote positivity, and produce beauty for the sake of beauty. Human artists bring intention, purpose, and personality to their art, reflecting the complexity and diversity of the human species.

Is there a possibility that the "human touch" in artwork will become less and less evident until one day, suddenly, it evaporates?

While AI *is* powerful, it is still just an augmentation of human creativity rather than a replacement. Humans have a wide range of qualities that make us distinct, such as empathy, intuition, and moral reasoning. These are impossible for AI for imitate.

As a human artist, you possess a remarkable gift -- the power of imagination. Your imagination is the fertile soil from which your artistic endeavors blossom and take flight. It is a wellspring of limitless potentialities waiting to be brought forth into the world. Your voice, your thoughts, and your ideas are unlike any other. As you navigate your creative journey, embrace the unfamiliar landscape. Adaptability and openness to new things are the keys that unlock doors to innovation and growth. Investigate new technologies, experiment with different mediums, and let the winds of change guide you toward uncharted territories. Remember, it is your willingness to evolve that keeps your artistic flame burning bright.

So, dear (human) artist, let your unique voice resound through your art, with our without AI. Embrace the power of your imagination, celebrate the richness of your experiences, and fearlessly share your creations with the world.

Your artistic spirit is a beacon of inspiration for others, forever reminding us that in this vast universe, there will always be human artists, shining their light and leaving an indelible mark on the canvas of existence.

And no robot can take that away.

Hello Artists!

If you enjoyed this book, please write us a review on Amazon!

We would love to hear from you!

Made in the USA
Middletown, DE
27 July 2023

35785536R00076